AMERICAN LEGENDS™

Davy Crockett

Marianne Johnston

The Rosen Publishing Group's
PowerKids Press™
New York

Published in 2001 by The Rosen Publishing Group, Inc.
29 East 21st Street, New York, NY 10010

First Edition

Book Design: Michael de Guzman

Photo Credits: p. 4 Painting of Davy Crockett by Robert Lindneux (1871–1970) © SuperStock; p. 7 © Paul Avis/FPG International; p. 8 © Pat O'Hara/CORBIS; pp. 11, 12, 16 © North Wind Picture Archives; p. 15 © D. Robert Franz/CORBIS; p. 19 Portrait of Davy Crockett by James H. Shegogue © National Portrait Gallery, Smithsonian Institution/Art Resource, NY; p. 20 © D. Boone/CORBIS.

Johnston, Marianne.
     Davy Crockett / Marianne Johnston.
        p. cm.— (American legends)
     Includes index.
     Summary: This book describes the life and the legend of Davy Crockett, a backwoodsman who became a frontier hero.
     ISBN 0-8239-5581-8
     1. Crockett, Davy, 1786–1836—Juvenile literature. 2. Pioneers—Tennessee—Biography—Juvenile literature. 3. Tennessee—Biography—Juvenile literature. 4. Legislators—United States—Biography—Juvenile literature. [1. Crockett, Davy, 1786–1836. 2. Pioneers. 3. Legislators.] I. Title. II. Series.
     2000
     976.8'04'092—dc21
     [B]

Manufactured in the United States of America

Contents

This picture by American artist Robert Lindneux shows Davy Crockett
wearing a coonskin cap and a fringed deerskin jacket.
Davy became known for his skills as a woodsman.

Davy Crockett

Davy Crockett lived from 1786 to 1836, when our nation was still young. He was a farmer, hunter, soldier, and politician. He was also an excellent woodsman. A woodsman is a person who is used to life in the woods and is skilled in hunting, fishing, and trapping. Over time, Davy's life grew into a **legend**. Today he is remembered as a pioneer hero.

Some people have said that he could tame wild animals just by looking at them. This means that he could make them gentle. Davy loved to tell tales and jokes. One time Davy said he swallowed a bolt of lightning. He even told a tale about riding an alligator up Niagara Falls!

What Is a Legend?

People all over the world honor legends. A legend is a story that has been passed down through the years. These stories may be true or they may be made up. Some legends are about people. Legends about people usually center on the qualities of a person that we respect. Qualities are the features that make that person special. The **legendary** Davy Crockett was brave, honest, and funny. Often, the stories about the legendary person are full of **exaggeration**. The tales usually change and get more amazing with each telling. These fun and interesting stories help people remember what was important about the legendary person.

It is fun to read legends, or stories that come down to us from the past. These stories are not always about real people or events from the past. Sometimes parts of the legends are made up to make the stories more interesting.

This cabin is at the Davy Crockett Birthplace State Park in Limestone, Tennessee. The cabin is much like the one in which Davy was born in 1786. The museum at the park also contains exhibits that tell about Davy's life as a hunter and Congressman.

Born in Tennessee

The real-life Davy Crockett was born on August 17, 1786, in what is now eastern Tennessee. Tennessee did not become a state until ten years after Davy was born. Davy's parents, John and Rebecca, had moved from North Carolina to Tennessee in 1783. Davy was the fifth of nine children. Davy's first boyhood home was on the banks of the Big Limestone River. Tree-covered mountains and beautiful green forests surrounded his home.

When Davy was eight years old, his father opened a tavern, or inn, where travelers could eat and spend the night. Many travelers, adventurers, and traders stayed at the Crocketts' inn. Davy heard many strange tales from these interesting travelers.

Davy's First Job

Davy's father put him to work when he was only 12. He sent his son to work for a man who was taking a herd of cattle to Virginia. Davy helped drive, or move, the herd more than 200 miles (321.9 km) from Tennessee to Virginia. The trip took about two weeks. After arriving at his home in Virginia, the **cattle driver** wanted Davy to keep working for him. Even though he was homesick, Davy worked for the man for about a month. Then Davy could not stand being away from home any longer. In the middle of a cold, snowy night, Davy sneaked out of the cattle driver's house. He got rides from travelers who were going in the direction of his home until he finally reached his family.

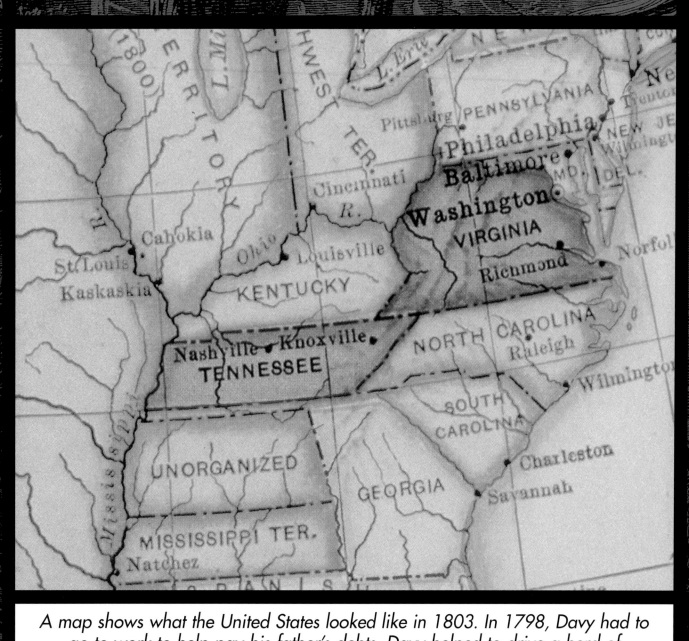

A map shows what the United States looked like in 1803. In 1798, Davy had to go to work to help pay his father's debts. Davy helped to drive a herd of cattle from Tennessee to Virginia when he was only 12 years old.

Like the hunters shown here, Davy hunted bears to help feed his family. Davy was a very good rifleman and liked to hunt in the backwoods.

Growing Up

Davy set out on his own at age 13. He walked hundreds of miles (km). He worked for cattle drivers and farmers in Virginia and Maryland. Life was often hard for him on the road. When he was 16, he returned home. Davy had not been to school for more than a few days in his whole life. Still, he had learned a lot about different people during his travels.

In 1806, Davy married Mary Finley. Everyone called her Polly. The Crocketts moved to a farm in Tennessee. Over the next few years, the couple had two sons. Davy hunted deer and bear to feed his family. He enjoyed hunting in the backwoods, the wooded areas where few people lived, and became known as a very good **rifleman**.

Tales of a Backwoodsman

Legend says that wild animals became tame around Davy. One story says that a bear made friends with the Crockett family. The animal would come inside the house and sit by the fireplace with Davy. It has been said that the bear helped churn, or stir, cream into butter and that he opened the door for Davy when he came home late!

The legendary Davy was also said to be able to get a raccoon down from a tree with a smile. He would stand by the tree and look up at the raccoon. He would smile widely and stare. He would not stop until the raccoon came down.

Davy often bragged that he could get a raccoon down from a tree by grinning at it. He once said he mistook the knot of a tree branch for a raccoon. He grinned at it for a long time and then found that he had grinned all the bark off of the tree!

The Creeks were angry at the white settlers for taking away their land. The white settlers attacked the Creeks first and started a war. Some people do not want to remember that the real Davy Crockett killed Native Americans in this war.

The Creek War

In 1811, the Crocketts moved across Tennessee. They made a new home near the border of Alabama. By 1813, white **settlers** in Alabama had angered the Native Americans living there. These Native Americans were named the Creeks. The Creeks were upset because the white settlers took away their land. Some of the settlers worried that the Creeks would attack them. They decided to attack the Creeks first. The Creeks fought back. This started a war. Davy helped fight against the Creeks. After Davy came home from the Creek war, Polly gave birth to a daughter. In the summer of 1815, Polly died. In 1816, Davy married Elizabeth Patton to care for his children.

Going to Washington

Backwoodsmen like Davy Crockett were becoming well known and important. In 1821, Davy was **elected** to the Tennessee **legislature**. In 1827, he was elected to the **House of Representatives** in **Congress**. Davy was in Congress from 1827 to 1831, and then again from 1833 to 1835. As a Congressman, he often made speeches and told stories about his adventures. Books came out filled with stories about Davy. A play called *The Lion of the West* was written in 1831. The **frontier** hero of the play might have been based on Davy. In 1834, Davy and Congressman Thomas Chilton from Kentucky wrote a book about Davy's life. Davy had become a legend while he was still living.

Davy served in Congress in Washington, D.C. He worked to pass laws for poor settlers, so that they could buy land at low prices.

CROCKETT

This monument honors the Texans who died at the Alamo. Legend says that Davy Crockett was killed while firing his favorite gun, Old Betsy. Even though they lost at the Alamo, the Texan settlers later won the revolution in April 1836.

The Texas Revolution

In 1835, Davy moved to Texas. At this time Texas was not yet a state. The 49-year-old Davy wanted to explore the American frontier. He joined the Texas army. He fought in the **Texas Revolution** in 1836. The revolution was a war against the Mexican government that ruled Texas. The settlers who lived in Texas wanted Texas to be free from Mexico. The most famous battle of the revolution was the battle at the Alamo. The Alamo was a fort in San Antonio, Texas. On March 6, 1836, a large army of Mexican soldiers attacked the small band of Texan soldiers at the Alamo. After a fierce battle, the Texans were beaten. Davy Crockett died in battle.

Remembering Davy Crockett

Today you can visit the place where Davy Crockett was born. It is called the Davy Crockett Birthplace State Park, and it is in Limestone, Tennessee. The museum there tells all about Davy Crockett's life. You can visit a log cabin that is set up to look like the one Davy lived in as a boy. Each year in August, the Crockett Celebration takes place in the park. The day is full of music, games, and barbecued food.

Davy Crockett is a great American legend. There are many books, movies, and songs about the legendary Davy Crockett. He will never be forgotten.

Glossary

cattle driver (KA-tul DRY-vur) A person who moves cattle from one place to another.

Congress (KOHN-gres) The part of the United States government that makes laws and is made up of the House of Representatives and the Senate. The members of Congress are chosen by the people of their states.

elected (ee-LEK-tid) Chosen for an office by voters.

exaggeration (ihg-zah-juh-RAY-shun) Something made to seem larger or more amazing than it really is.

frontier (frun-TEER) The edge of a settled country, where the wilderness begins.

House of Representatives (HOWS OV reh-prih-ZEN-tuh-tivs) A part of Congress, the law-making body of the government of the United States.

legend (LEH-jend) A story passed down through the years that many people believe.

legendary (LEH-jen-der-ee) To be based on a legend or to be famous.

legislature (LEH-juh-slay-chur) A group of elected people that have the power to make the laws of a state or country.

rifleman (RY-ful-man) A person who is good at shooting a rifle, a type of large gun.

settlers (SEH-tuh-lers) People who move to a new land to live.

Texas Revolution (TEX-is REH-vuh-loo-shun) The name of the war fought by Texan settlers against the Mexican government.

Index

Web Sites

To learn more about Davy Crockett, check out these Web sites:
http://www.americanwest.com/pages/davycroc.htm
http://www.lsjunction.com/people/crockett.htm